POCKET GUIDE TO

Riches

POCKET GUIDE TO

Riches

A Formula to Create Money On a Consistent Basis

SUSIE GREENE

BALBOA.
PRESS

A DIVISION OF HAY HOUSE

Balboa Press books may be ordered through booksellers or by contacting:

Balboa Press
A Division of Hay House
1663 Liberty Drive
Bloomington, IN 47403
www.balboapress.com
1-(877) 407-4847

Because of the dynamic nature of the Internet, any web addresses or
links contained in this book may have changed since publication and
may no longer be valid. The views expressed in this work are solely those
of the author and do not necessarily reflect the views of the publisher,
and the publisher hereby disclaims any responsibility for them.

The author of this book does not dispense medical advice or prescribe the use
of any technique as a form of treatment for physical, emotional, or medical
problems without the advice of a physician, either directly or indirectly. The
intent of the author is only to offer information of a general nature to help
you in your quest for emotional and spiritual well-being. In the event you use
any of the information in this book for yourself, which is your constitutional
right, the author and the publisher assume no responsibility for your actions.

Any people depicted in stock imagery provided by Thinkstock are models,
and such images are being used for illustrative purposes only.
Certain stock imagery © Thinkstock.

ISBN: 978-1-4525-3242-4 (sc)
ISBN: 978-1-4525-3243-1 (e)

Library of Congress Control Number: 2011901166

Printed in the United States of America

Balboa Press rev. date: 2/4/2011

To Andrew, the beautiful Being who showed up in this life as my son.

ACKNOWLEDGEMENTS

I would like to express my love and gratitude to the following people.

To the kind staff of Balboa Press and my publishing consultant, Joanie Schaublin, for her infectious enthusiasm and positive and loving support in the creation of this book.

To a beautiful angel named Cori Maas, whose words of encouragement uplifted me more that she will ever know.

For my long list of prosperity teachers who have inspired and influenced me including John Randolph Price, Catherine Ponder, Napoleon Hill, Wallace Wattles, Jerry and Esther Hicks, Dr. Joe Vitale, Edwene Gaines, Terry Cole Whittaker, Louise Hay, Charles Fillmore, Bob Proctor, Michael Bernard Beckwith, John and Barbara Waterhouse.

A special thanks for my dear friend Davon Embler, who supported me through the positive changes in my life and reminded me that my soul was on its right and perfect path. I love you.

CONTENTS

FOREWORD

I met Susie in 1988 at a casting call for an independent film I was directing in Asheville, NC. I knew the moment I saw her that she was not only a good actress, but there was much more behind this gentle spirit with the reddish blonde hair. Susie and I became friends and over the years I have seen her grow leaps and bounds in her spiritual life. She is clear, honest and funny. Her simplicity is genuine and therefore makes *"Pocket Guide To Riches/A Formula To Create Money On A Consistent Basis"* easy to read, easy to understand, and easy to practice. Everyone should read this book if you're looking to manifest a better life, be it money, health, love, joy, or friendships. Susie's *"Pocket Guide To Riches/A Formula To Create Money On A Consistent Basis"* will guide you to make clear decisions and open yourself up to the vast abundance of the Universe. It teaches the art of being grateful and will put you on the road to achieving your desires.

Marcia Flowers
Writer/Director
WhiteFlower Entertainment Productions

INTRODUCTION

For well over two decades, I've been on a spiritual journey, studying metaphysics and the Laws of the Universe in every way possible.. the Law of Attraction, Science of Mind, Abraham, Unity principles, and any thing else I could get my hands on. I've done it all. Meditation, workshops, retreats, I've read books, chanted, changed my thinking, heck, even walked on fire. But something was missing. I still just couldn't grasp what everyone was talking about as far as riches. You know, the big Cha-Ching! Creating money. Manifesting abundance. But a year ago, I had one of those a-ha moments that stops you in your tracks. So, I began journaling all that was coming to me, coming *through* me, and created a "formula" that began to change my life.

At first, I was in a bit of shock! Things were shifting so quickly, it was hard to keep up! In a month I was exhilarated, and in ninety days, I was on my knees, with tears of joy and awe at was happening in my life. It was unbelievable! Magical!

Money was flowing to me in amazing ways! I'd go to my online bank account, and *unexpected* deposits would be there. Deposits I did not make! I got calls on a consistent basis for work...work I love to do! I received expected checks in the mail, I received *unexpected* checks in the mail. I received Visa gift cards in the mail...it goes on and on. But it wasn't just money. It was Divine ideas. Ideas towards creating my life in a way that I never would have anticipated, filled with passion and joy. And people and circumstances were showing up to support those ideas. And the more I focused on the "formula" I had created, the more my wealth grew....and continues to grow.

I knew that I had to share this. I did not set out to create a "formula" much less write a book, but by opening myself up to this All- Providing Substance, it has unfolded in a beautiful and miraculous way. And in the sharing of it, it *is* the Divine Idea, the Divine Plan.

It doesn't matter how little you have right now, in this moment. It doesn't matter if you have NO money. It doesn't matter what circumstances you have created, if you're young or old, educated or uneducated. It doesn't matter what your religious beliefs are. THIS FORMULA WORKS.

Ernest Holmes says, "There is a Power in the Universe and you *must* use it." This is our work to do. Our only job on this planet is to express God. Express Good. Period. It is our *duty* to live a life of joy and *huge abundance.*

According to Emmet Fox ("Mental Equivalents") it is our duty to demonstrate. Why? Because you have to prove the harmony of Being in your own life. If there were no need to demonstrate, or express God or Good, we may as well go to bed and stay there.

This is a book that will teach you how to create money on a consistent basis. It's not a get rich quick scheme. It's the real thing. Powerful. Successful. To manifest *all* good things in your life.

However, you have to commit to doing the work. It's a simple process, but like anything, it won't work, if you don't DO the work. This is a magical formula. It will change your life! As surely as you breathe, money will flow to you! Get excited....get very excited! And get ready for money to show up in ways you can't imagine!

By now, you have probably heard of the Law of Attraction.

The techniques that are presented in this book, are techniques that when combined with the Law of Attraction, are extremely powerful.

Now, granted, there are probably a million books already written on the subject of how to get more out of life and how to become rich. And this material certainly will not be the last word written or spoken. However, if you will truly focus on these principles, learn them and *apply* them, and you open yourself up to this all providing God energy Substance, with just a little practice, you will be living a life of riches that show up for you in magical ways, on a continuous basis. Where there was once lack and limitation, there is only prosperous, rich, demonstrations in your life.

I truly believe we are ALL a channel for one another's good. And the good of the whole truly does begin with the individual. So.....let's get started.

THE IMPORTANCE OF A SIMPLE DECISION

To help you to understand my big "a-ha" moment, let's go back a little to explain how this all came about.

As long as I can remember, I've been an actress. At 5 years old, I would go into my parents' closet, put on their clothes to create some silly costume, and come out as a zany character to entertain them.

In high school, I joined the drama club and by the end of my senior year was writing plays and traveling with the club to perform award winning competitions. I was also voted "class clown." No, not the "prettiest" or "most likely to succeed!" Just the funny girl. But I didn't mind. I enjoyed making people laugh, though it mostly only served to get me in trouble in the classroom.

By the time I reached my early 20's, I decided to head out to Los Angeles to pursue an acting career, where

I lived for 7 years. I didn't have huge success, but I did spend a lot of money on workshops, portfolios, agents, classes, headshots, etc! In 1988 I moved back to Asheville, NC, my hometown, still pursuing the acting. I was in every play I could possibly audition for, many local commercials, and small gigs here and there. But still, nothing substantial.

In 1996....and here's where it gets interesting, I remember standing in the kitchen with my father and he looked at me and said, "Susie, if you haven't made it as an actress by now, you're never going to!"

Wow. Talk about devastated. Acting was my life! Well, as much as that comment hurt me, it really ticked me off! The nerve! That night, alone in my room, through the tears, I made a vow to myself to succeed. I didn't know how or when, but I'd show him! And I vividly remember thinking...this is it! I WILL be successful.

A month later, a Tide commercial audition came to town. A big New York director and crew came to Asheville! It was a major cattle call for auditions....in the newspapers, radio, TV, etc. Three hundred people auditioned for this commercial. I was one of the handful of lucky people to be cast. Me! The girl who had spent all that time in LA and a summer in New York at the American Academy of Dramatic Arts, with no real success, had finally found success in her own back yard!!

Of course my parents were elated. They said, "Susie, we knew you could do it!! We're so proud of you!" I thought to myself, 'Who are you? And what have you done with my parents?!'

Well, $30,000 later, my dad never said another word!! The work continued...other national commercials, movie bits, etc.

Now, lets go back to the spiritual a-ha aspect of all of this. In the year of 2000, I discovered Unity Church and shortly after that, the Church of Religious Science. The philosophies of these churches stated that our thoughts are things and that what you think about, you bring about. That what you think on and focus on, you bring into your life. Me, being the good student that I am...I am coach-able, began to practice these principles.

A year ago, I started thinking about that Tide commercial. I even discussed it with a friend, trying to figure it out.

I had no clue in 1996 of any positive thinking techniques, or tricks, or theories, or spiritual principles of any kind. I did not know anything about creating my experience through thought. I didn't know one thing about *deliberately* creating whatsoever! So, I started wondering....what was it that created that success? What did I do? How did I do it? I certainly wasn't *conscious* or aware of any deliberate creating!

And then, it hit me like a ton of bricks!! Something so simple, so fundamental.....I FINALLY made the connection.

What happened that night my father told me I'd never make it, is that I got so angry...that I **DECIDED** to become successful. I distinctly remember "making up my mind" with such conviction....and with such *emotion,* that there was absolutely no doubt in my mind that it already WAS. Period. I would accept nothing less.

Now, this concept is nothing new. It's what Wayne Dyer calls 'The Power of Intention.' Charles Fillmore, in his book, *Prosperity*, calls it 'mental determination'. Napoleon Hill in his book *Think and Grow Rich*, calls it 'burning desire.' It's choice. We choose. We decide. We get clear.

But having this epiphany, I started using it on a daily basis. For example, if I was in the grocery store, and that inner talk would say, 'you can't afford that, Susie.' I would remember the power of decision. I would consciously *decide* in that store that I was rich, and I could have that expensive item. I knew that whatever I decided in that moment, *would be my life.* My experience. It never failed, after making this decision, something would show up as my good, whether it was a check, potential work, a friend called to take me to lunch....it was unlimited!

At one point I even got a knock at my door. It was a young man who worked with the cable company that provided my Internet service. He proceeded to ask me if I was Ms. Greene. Then he asked, are you paying "x" amount of dollars for your internet service? Yes, was my reply. He then began to explain that I was paying too much money and they could lower my monthly bill!!! I'm sure I had to pick my jaw up off of the porch! When does any cable or utility company of *any* kind tell you that you are paying too much and volunteer to lower your bill?! Things like this just make me laugh. It's like a delightful surprise from the Universe! When I regained consciousness, I invited him in and we made the changes! Fun, fun!

When you decide something, you are setting up a "vibration." Everything in this Universe is made up of energy. You, me, the trees, the chair you're sitting on, the stars…. And since energy is actually vibration, that means that everything that exists vibrates. Everything!

You're thinking, what does this have to do with me? Because since we're all energy, and since we're all vibrating every moment of every day, the energy that flows from us comes from our highly formed *emotions* to create highly charged electromagnetic wave patterns of energy…. making us powerful, walking magnets! In a nutshell…it's the Law of Attraction. So, the electromagnetic vibrations you send out every moment of every day is what you are bringing into your life, big or small, good or bad, negative or positive…everything! No exceptions!

So when you make the decision to be rich….and you get excited about it, you are telling the Universe the way it is! You make the decision to *feel* rich. That's what you're vibrating and what ever you're vibrating, you're attracting.

You are vibrating at different frequencies, and the Universe will *match* that frequency. It *must* give you what you're feeling and what you're decreeing! It's the Universal law. You are essentially, directing energy!

The first step to any achievement, is that you make the conscious choice, or decision first, to have, be, or do something. You set it up from the get go. And with everything in your being, you believe it to be true. You accept no less. When you do this, you automatically set into motion this vibration, this life force energy that creates worlds.

It's no different when you decide that you can't afford something. The Universe will give you what you have just decreed for yourself. You are constantly making decisions. Why not make the decision to *have* money, to afford? You do this every single day...every moment, you're making a decision. *And the Universe gives you what you decide.*

Life does not care whether you call yourself rich or poor, strong or weak. It will eternally reward you with what ever you decree for yourself as true.

I recently heard a friend say that she heard that if you call certain medical offices and tell them that you are having a hardship that they will give you a discount. Why do I want to make a decision and declare for myself that I'm in hardship? This will only create more hardship! This is what you are setting up for yourself!

I can't tell you how important this first step is. You must start making positive, rich decisions in your mind. YOU are the captain of your own ship. YOU are the master of your own mind. YOU are the creator of your own experience.... through every single decision you make.

And here's the kicker. The Universe, Substance, *wants* to express riches through you. This living Substance is always moving toward more life and fuller functioning. It wants to give you money, or anything else you desire. But you have to have the courage to decide first. *You have to have the faith to decide and decree it so.* This God stuff, this Substance is waiting to bring something into form because that's its job. Your job is to decide what it will be... and it will lovingly give you what you decide. Period.

Psychologists say, "When one is truly ready for a thing...it puts in it's appearance."

This Substance is a Living Presence. It is Intelligent. It MUST expand and express its fullness. And it MUST do this through YOU. It can ONLY do this through you. You see, we are the instrument for this Divine Power to do its work. It is forever expanding and fulfilling Itself through us.

And one last thing before we move on to the next step. Never, ever, ever spend in fear. If you are having a battle with your inner talk, should I or shouldn't I, can I afford it or not, and you buy that thing and you feel fearful about it. STOP. You're doing yourself more harm than good. You must get to a place where you *feel* rich. Where you feel confident in making your decision to be rich.

In fact, the very *way*, the very attitude, in which you spend your money is very important.

By spending our money in the energy of fear, we are focusing on the "not having" of money, and we are only attracting more inharmonious results and more lack. We must learn to spend it joyfully and positively, understanding that money is *energy*.

Joe Vitale, in his book, *Attract Money Now,* calls this "prosperous spending." Our very mindset of money when we are spending it will determine future demonstrations in our life. In other words, the positive feelings and emotions that prosperous spending brings is what brings more positive things into our life. Spending our money in fear or even *guilt* will only bring more scarcity and lack into our life.

Have you ever bought something and felt guilty for it? I know that in my own life, I have felt the "guilt" of buying something nice for myself. These are just the old tapes that come up from the many years of conditioning from the stories of lack from parents, society, etc. If this happens to you, be gentle with yourself! Change is a process! Then get back to being clear that you are working with a Power that supports you in enjoying your life and all its gifts! Get excited that you are buying something to nurture you! You deserve it! And give yourself permission to enjoy it. The joy of spending your money is tied to giving, even if it is giving to *yourself.*

It's the same with your bills. Do not pay one bill in fear. If you have a strong emotional, "knot in your stomach" feeling when you are paying bills, STOP. Meditate. Be still. Get peaceful about it. KNOW that you are taken care of and that all of your needs are met. Get into an "appreciation" state of being. You appreciate that you have electricity, right? You appreciate and are grateful for your water, for the ability to get on the internet, phone, TV, etc! Show the Universe how grateful you are!

Claim your power....own it! Jump in to the void. Decide! Know! Have Faith! If you do this, I guarantee things will shift for you. You must COMMAND the thing you desire from this Living Presence. The word *command* means to have authority, to have control. You must take control, decide what you want and command its appearance! This, with FAITH and GRATITUDE will manifest ANYTHING you desire in your life.

Money WILL show up. Because you have declared to the universe that this is how it is!! Your good will come to you in ways that you couldn't even have imagined. I received a refund check from the state that was automatically deposited into my checking account! I have no idea what this refund was for. But it came a day after I declared that I could indeed afford something, made the decision, bought it, and felt empowered by it.

You are a spiritual Being expressing God. You know with all your soul that you are taken care of and now that you have made the decision to be rich, the Universe, that unseen Life Force energy, this Intelligence, WILL support you. This is where you want to be emotionally. Then, as you stand in that store aisle, something inside you shifts. You actually get excited! Excited that you are in control! You are the power! Yea! Now buy that item!

When you make a decision to honor your soul and you take action to back up the decision, this Divine Power, this Living Presence will rally behind you to support your efforts.

And here's the fun part! The more you claim and decide and hold the consciousness that you are rich, the more experiences you have of money. Money starts to flow... and you say, "Hey, I receive money every few days!" And every few days, you receive money. You keep declaring it, it keeps showing up. It keeps showing up *because* you keep declaring it. It's a beautiful *partnership* with the Divine. You have tapped in to this Life Force Energy and you are now co-creating with it.

And then...in that moment you realize...Your life has suddenly become...."*magical.*"

AFFIRMATIONS

With courage and conviction, I now decide to be rich.

It is my choice to be rich, and the
Universe supports my decision.

I now make positive, rich decisions and have faith
in the invisible Substance to fill all my desires.

I COMMAND my good here and now and know this
Invisible Substance MUST express through me.

I spend money in joy and enthusiasm, knowing
my supply is endless and immediate.

Thou shalt decree a thing, and it shall be
established unto thee. (Job 22:28)

YOUR DIVINE PARTNER
WORKING WITH SUBSTANCE

I want to talk about a little itty bitty thing called Substance. What is substance? Webster says that substance is ultimate reality that underlies all outward manifestations; a kind of matter. It is the Greek word for "stand under."

Jesus called it the Kingdom of the Heavens. Ernest Holmes states that Spirit is Substance and Substance is *supply*. Metaphysicians describe Substance as "mind essence." Science says it is the ether. Ether, being described as the upper region of space, the heavens. In the theory of light, that which permeates all space.

The word substance could be translated into many other words or phrases. Source, Source Energy, Divine Essence, Divine Intelligence, Life Force Energy. Call it what you will.

For the last ten years of my spiritual journey, I had not heard the word "substance" referred to very often. But in the last year, it seemed that every book I picked up talked about nothing BUT "Substance!"

So I began to pay attention.

When I began to focus only on "substance" things began to shift. By communicating directly with Substance, I began to have remarkable results. I began documenting the demonstrations and manifestations. Sometimes, I would have money show up within half an hour of focusing on my oneness with Substance, the all of all, and feeling that full, rich presence.

It's the God stuff that is absolutely the key to Prosperity.

Charles Fillmore states in his book "Prosperity":

> *This inexhaustible mind substance is available at all times and in all places to those who have learned to lay hold of it in consciousness. The spiritual substance from which comes all visible wealth is never depleted. It is right with you all the time and responds to your faith in it and your demand upon it.*

Hold that you are One with the all-providing substance and your prosperity runneth over! You are One with the all of all. You are One with the earth, the sky, the stars, the trees, the animals, the planets, the galaxy...everything. Just *feel* your oneness with it. As you begin to feel consciously "at one" or unified with this all providing substance, it will begin to well up within you, a feeling of fullness, and overflow into your affairs. Practice this daily! Do not let one day go by that you do not sit quietly and focus on your oneness with Substance.

I began daily to affirm "Divine Substance is the one and only reality." It's the only thing that exists. There truly is no such thing as "lack."

You must get in the habit of *relying* only on substance, and focus only on substance every single day with every breath you take. Substance. it's the all of all, everything that is. It's in the ethers all around you. It's this God stuff waiting to be brought into form. And with your mighty and clear decision, and your all-knowing FAITH in Substance, it *will* show up in form!

What I have come to understand is that when you begin to focus on substance, this all providing supply, and you take your focus off of money, what is really happening is that you're not focusing on your fear or lack of money, thereby creating that emotional negative energy that *blocks* your money from coming to you. When you begin to only focus on substance, and you get to that feeling place of fullness, and you really begin to feel happy and excited, this is the secret to attracting your good.

This is a most important lesson to learn. When we focus on money, we oftentimes associate it with "not having" and then our energy around money is negative. This only brings unhappy, unfulfilled results.

The more conscious you become of the PRESENCE OF THE LIVING SUBSTANCE, the more it will manifest itself for you. No matter who you are and what your immediate need, you can demonstrate this law. If your thoughts are confused, become still and know. Know that you are one with the Substance of all that exists.

This unfailing Substance is ALWAYS ready to give! It must give, for that is its nature. But you must be ready to accept it.

Never underestimate the power of Substance. Begin to work with it every day, rely on it, have faith in Substance and only Substance. Open yourself up to this all-providing Substance. Concentrate on it daily. It will be happy to work with you, for you, and through you, to provide for you in every way and bring prosperity into your life.

3 Elements to Working with Substance

I. E. A.

1. IMAGINATION
2. EMOTION
3. APPRECIATION

Now that you have an understanding of Substance and you have begun to focus on it as being the one and only reality and your supply, there are three elements to working with substance.

Imagination, Emotion, and Appreciation.

IMAGINATION

Let's start with imagination.

Scientists are now beginning to understand the imaging faculties of the mind. They declare that imagination is one of the most powerful uses of the mind.

To quote our friend Charles Fillmore again:

> *The imagination is a wonderful creative power. It builds all things out of the one Substance. When you associate it with faith, you make things just as real as those that God makes, for imagination is a co-creator with God. Whatever you form in the mind, and have faith in, will become substantial!*

Your imagination is an incredibly powerful tool. Use this power to let your mind play! Your subconscious mind cannot differentiate what is fantasy and what is real. So whatever you hold in your mind to be true, and have faith in, WILL BECOME SUBSTANTIAL!

There is a concept called Fantasy, Theory, Fact. Think about it. Everything that exists, that was ever invented, was first fantasy... imagination. An idea in the mind of man. Then what happened? What ever that idea was, it then became theory...then fact! Not that long ago, carrying around a pocket sized device that plays 200 songs, or a small instrument that is a movie and music player, an e-reader and internet accessible, or even landing on the moon was sheer fantasy! Those who dared to imagine it held to the vision, boldly made it theory, and wa-lah! It became fact....real.

Every great leader, or millionaire, was first a dreamer who first had a certain amount of dreaming, desiring and planning before they acquired money. If you do not SEE YOURSELF WITH GREAT RICHES, in your imagination, you will never see them in your bank account.

Henry Ford, poor and uneducated, dreamed of a horseless carriage. He believed in his idea and would not give up even when it took years for his team to build it.

Thomas Edison who had only a few months of schooling, dreamed of a lamp that could be run by electricity, and despite ten thousand failures, did not give up until his dream was a reality.

Despite her greatest misfortune, Helen Keller's entire life is evidence that no one is defeated until they accept it for themselves. We are all capable of amazing success.

Dare to fantasize a better life! One filled with money, gold, riches, and what ever your imagination can produce. Your imagination is going to evoke the *emotional* connection you need to tap in to this creative energy.

Begin to write down your desires. This will enable you to make the mental connection with Substance. For every thing that you write down, see yourself as having it. Feel how it feels to have it, to do it, or to be it. If you can imagine it, and lay hold of it in your mind, those images will show up in form! THIS IS THE LAW! You are making a "mental image" of your desire and impressing it upon your subconscious mind. When making your list, don't just write what you think you should have, or what would be nice to have to get by. Dare to dream big. What do you really want? Why settle for so little when you can have so much? You can have whatever you can imagine yourself having. Believe, and begin to have a mental image of your success. Visualize having or being or doing *as if* you already have it! Be the actor in your own script...worthy of winning an Academy Award!!

Then, in your imagination, and seeing yourself as having, being or doing what you desire, *get excited!* You know that it already *is.* YEA!

Jump up and down in your living room, shouting, "Thank you, Substance! Thank you, God! Thank you, thank you, thank you!" And *imagine* your good showing up. Know your good is showing up! Which brings us to our second element:

EMOTION

There are many teachers and philosophies that stress the importance of our thoughts. And our thoughts are indeed important and are "things." But it's the *feelings* or *emotions* behind our desire that propels this Life Force Energy into gear and demonstrates it at lightning speed.

The Universe loves speed, and when combined with your DECISION, your FAITH and your EXCITEMENT and HAPPINESS, the Universe must and will demonstrate for you. This is Law. We create by *feeling*.

In his book, "Think and Grow Rich," Napoleon Hill writes,

> *"All THOUGHTS which have been emotionalized, (given emotion to) and mixed with FAITH, begin immediately to translate themselves into their physical equivalent. The emotions, or the "feeling" aspect of thoughts are what give thoughts vitality, life and action."*

Emotion is extremely important to connect to your imagination and visualizations. The vision you build in your conscious mind is built with your imagination. When you turn your vision over to your emotional mind, you're connecting up to the entire universe and this is the part that the average person on the street just doesn't get. When we talk about emotion we are really talking about Universal Intelligence, that part of us where the spiritual essence of ourselves takes over.

So when you make the decision to be rich, and you make a mental image in your mind of your desire....and you get EXCITED about it, you are telling your subconscious mind the way it is and you are making the connection with the Higher Intelligence.

Remember, what ever you're vibrating, you're attracting. And emotion is vibration!! It's the Universal law. It *must* give you what you're *feeling* and what you're decreeing!

A friend of mine told me that she can easily create money when she's in a crisis. I asked her why that is? She said because she feels that it's about her fear and as a result, her *determination* of creating money. What I translate that to mean is that in her highly charged emotion of fear, she makes a demand on the Universe. And in that demand, she is *deciding* that money come to her now. Substance responds to it and speeds the process up...because in her fear, she's got some mighty powerful energy behind it; her highly charged, electromagnetic energy! Not unlike my anger with my dad in the kitchen, and the determination that followed.

So, I asked my friend, don't you think you could just as easily create money on a consistent basis by getting *excited* every day? That too is a powerful emotion, if you really, genuinely can evoke that. Plus, you'll be a lot happier and your day will be in perfect alignment with who you really are. When this happens, and you are in that alignment, everything flows perfectly. Haven't you had days like that, when everything just seemed to fall into your lap and synchronicity was everywhere present? Do you know that every day could be like that? It could if we decide and decree it so! Also, the overall benefits of being in that high energy, will improve your health, your relationships, your financial well being, and more of the things you want in your life will be attracted *to you.*

Emotion is a powerful creator of *anything* you desire in your life.

My sister had been trying to sell her house for two years. Her husband is in the Air Force, so, they had to leave their home in Georgia and move to Arizona. The house in Georgia stayed on the market, on and off, renters came, renters went. More problems...on and on. All of this on top of having to pay the two mortgages for both homes. After two years, they finally had a buyer. The loan was approved, the contracts were signed, the closing day was to arrive. At the last minute, the buyer decided that she no longer wanted to buy the house. My sister was devastated. And weary. And frustrated. And angry!

I shared with her my formula and asked her, "what do you really want?" knowing the answer of course. She said, "To sell my house!!" "OK, then stop thinking about this woman who fell through and being angry with her. You're giving all your energy and power to her and to a situation that's going nowhere. Instead focus on what you *want.* Focus on the *right* buyer. Make a *decision* to sell the house and SEE IT SOLD! Visualize the perfect couple buying your house and get *exited* about it....accept nothing else." I encouraged her to get so excited that she jump up and down in her living room. My sister thinks I'm nuts!

A week later, I got the call from my sister. A couple who had been trying to buy a house in foreclosure, but the deal had fallen through, were desperate to find a home. They happened to be driving around the neighborhood and saw the "For Sale" sign in the yard. They never hesitated, they *knew* this house was the home they had been looking for.

After two years of frustration and hopelessness, just a simple shift in consciousness created success for my sister! (I know she jumped around in her living room!) By focusing on what she wanted, affirming it, believing it and getting excited about it, she created the fulfillment of her desire in one week!

One last note. If you focus your attention on your desires, or even affirm something a million times a day, but do not mix EMOTION and FAITH with your words, you will not have satisfying results. This is a fact of huge importance, and one that most people do not understand, that thoughts and making affirmations alone will not give desirable results.

Plain, unemotional words will not influence the subconscious mind. And here's the tricky part. You can't pretend. You must conjure up a sincere, genuine feeling of emotion. The only way to do this is PERSISITENCE.

Keep affirming, keep BELIEVING and KNOWING and get EXCITED and PASSIONATE about your desire. Don't worry if you cannot master this at first. Just persist and practice, practice, practice!

Lastly, let's not forget our remaining element:

APPRECIATION

An attitude of gratitude will always invoke the Law of Abundance!

Being in an appreciative state is a "high frequency" emotion. It's much like the emotion of love. They are both the same vibration, the same energy. When you are in a state of appreciation, you *feel* good, you feel happy, light, and this is a high vibratory frequency that will bring more positive, magical demonstrations.

In John Randolph Price's "The Abundance Book", he writes:

> *Love life and every physical manifestation of life, and as you do, begin to express gratitude for the good that is yours now...for the infinite blessings of God, and for the solution to every problem and the fulfillment of every need. Feel the joy that is rising up in you...that's the vibration that will keep you in tune with all the channels of your good.*

When you choose to be in the energy of appreciation, and you are connected with your heart, with your soul, authentically and genuinely, that energy will manifest into physical abundance.

In Catherine Ponder's book, "Dare to Prosper," she states that when you give your appreciation to Substance, it seems to work overtime for you. She further writes:

Perhaps you wonder why it's important to have appreciation towards money. Money is filled with the Intelligence of the Universe. It reacts to your attitudes about it. It is a Law that you attract what you appreciate and repel what you depreciate.

Money responds accordingly. If you think favorably about money, it will increase and multiply for you. If you criticize it in any form, you literally dissipate and repel it from you.

One of the "magical" components of expressing your appreciation is that you are setting your mind to believe that what you have asked for is already so. This, in conjunction with this high vibration of loving and appreciative energy, is a power house of manifestation!

By expressing your appreciation and saying "thank you," for what you have asked for *before* you have received it, you have become definite in your prosperity and you are now in alignment to receive the thing you have given thanks for. You are ever receiving that which you are *being or seeing* yourself as already having. When you come into the joy of thanksgiving, you have already ACCEPTED your request as being true, and your FAITH is now the substance for bringing your desire.

Daily, as I meditate upon Substance, I joyfully express my gratitude and appreciation for Substance. "Thank you, thank you, Substance! I so appreciate you for showing up here and now in Rich Abundance!"

AFFIRMATIONS

Divine Substance is the one and only reality in my life.

Divine Substance, the all of all, now fills me up
with a feeling of fullness, richness, and peace.

Divine Substance now supplies my every demand.
I have faith and know that my good is here now.

I draw into my mind the very Substance
of Spirit. This substance is my supply and
shows up now in rich, appropriate form.

I now lay hold of all my good in consciousness,
therefore it shows up in form.

"Thank you, Substance! I so appreciate you for
showing up here and now in Rich Abundance!"

THE ART OF ALLOWING

I believe one of the most challenging things for us to learn about money, is how to *allow* it in.

Allowing is nothing more than giving up resistance. What is resistance? Fear, doubt, worry, resentment, anger, concern and any other negative emotion that we produce.

These negative emotions literally BLOCK our good and our money from flowing in. They put us in a lower frequency of vibration. We want to raise our vibration with loving, positive, feel good thoughts and feelings!

We worry about our rent being paid. We worry that we will be unable to pay our bills. We worry about what will happen next month. Fear, fear, fear! We've all been there. Unless we were born a Rockefeller! But this is the part where you have to go back to understanding who you are. YOU are the Power, remember? YOU DECIDE if you are rich or poor. YOU DECIDE what your life is...you set it up!

We are learning that we have a direct connection to Life, and this Life Force Energy, this All Knowing Substance, *responds* to us as we see ourselves.

Let me share with you a particular experience I had in coming to a "block."

I was going along, happily, creating money on a consistent basis, feeling as if I were walking on air. I constantly repeated, "Life is so good!" "My life is so good!" Then, suddenly, one of my buttons was pushed. Someone close to me made a comment to me that sent me to an angry, resentful place. I was frustrated, mostly because it took me out of my good feeling place. And I have enough experience to know that it's the "good feeling place" that attracts all good things into your life.

But try as I might, I could not get out of the "negative space" I was in. (which of course, was something for me to take a look at as far as my own issues). The anger and resentment soon turned into fear, worry and doubt, all of which I knew were resistant to my good. They are all negative emotions. They all vibrate at the same frequency. AND, they all attract more of the same.

So, as a result, my flow STOPPED!

This was a powerful lesson for me to understand how our negative emotions will spiral us downward, from one negative emotion to another, and block our good from coming.

The energy of money, or any good thing that you desire in your life, must supported by *love*. Furthermore, your money will not come to you if you are participating in criticism, verbal abuse, resentment, gossip or words of hatred of any kind. It simply cannot. This emotional whirlpool does not create the higher vibration that is necessary to attract it.

The first time I heard about the Law of Forgiveness and the role that forgiveness played in attracting money, I decided to put it to the test! The best place I believed for me to start was with my ex-husband! At the time, I was a single mom and was supposed to be receiving child support. Well, that child support came infrequently and sometimes not at all. Or it was an amount that was less than agreed upon. So, I began a daily ritual of forgiving this man. Forgiving all the past hurts, forgiving all the things that had not met my expectations in the relationship and forgiving the lack of child support.

I truly got to a place where I didn't care if I received another dime. I knew that this was not my source anyway. All-providing God Substance is. And this man was doing the best he could. Low and behold, within a few weeks of practicing forgiveness and letting it all go, I received a phone call from my ex, VOLUNTEERING to raise my child support amount! Not only did he keep his word in raising the amount, but it was never late again.

If we hold in consciousness anything against anyone, we are attracting disharmony in our own life. We must release everyone of all judgment, blame and condemnation to free ourselves.

Now, I don't advocate that we can be in a happy, loving state of being in every moment of every day. And there will always be the challenges that we *attract* into our life in order for us to grow and understand that we are Powerful Spiritual Beings on our path of evolvement. However, when you are aware that your thoughts and emotions, whether they are negative or positive, will be attracting the same, you're a lot more willing to let go of the negativity, and with practice, are able to move through the doubt, worry, and fear, more quickly and more lovingly. Your abundance is a direct response to your vibration. Your Love vibration!

Another idea to our resistance of allowing in money is that we have been conditioned that we have to work hard and struggle for it....that money does not grow on trees!

But your abundance is also a response to your BELIEF. So if you believe that your abundance comes only by way of work or action or struggle, then so be it. You have "decided" that. You have decreed it. If you say that you are on a "fixed" income, you have decided that.

But you can just as easily create money by *allowing* it in. Your well being or financial success is nothing you have to *earn* or work for. Granted, work is a wonderful channel for money to come to you. But that's all it is. A channel. The Universe has *many* channels for money to come to you, when you have no limitations on what those channels are.

You are not "making" something happen. You are "allowing" it.

In a book called "Dialogue on Awakening, Communion with a Loving Brother" Tom Carpenter has direct communication with Jesus as He channels through him. Jesus says:

> *"What I would encourage you to understand is that your financial limitations exists because you do not accept that money flows to you as easily as your belief allows it to happen."*

Wow! Read and re-read this. Our money flows to us as FREELY as we ALLOW it to happen.

So how do we allow it? By getting quiet, still and consciously allow all of our good to flow. We consciously make the connection with this all providing Substance and allow ourselves to have, be or do a thing. We take out of the equation all fear, doubt, worry, or concern of any kind. We know with all of our being that we are One with this Divine Living Presence that fills all our needs in EVERY way. Daily focus and speak aloud that you now allow in all of your good. Make that connection with Substance and let it fill you up!

You must have complete faith and trust in this invisible, unfailing, all providing Substance. THERE IS NOTHING ELSE.

Lack does not exist. You're only "job" is to understand this and to have faith in it. Just open yourself up to this Life Force Energy, this Supreme Intelligence. Rely upon it for *everything*. Your money, your health, your work, your relationships, your joy, your peace, your passion, your wisdom, your love; everything. Everything tangible and everything intangible. It's all that exists.

Everything to fulfill your experience is present when you have NO LIMITATIONS on receiving it!

Instead of "earning" abundance, "allow" abundance. Your work is just a channel for money...you can have MANY channels! And if money is not coming to you from your usual or known channels, ask for unusual channels to open up.

And in the allowing of your good, know that you may be guided to take action in some particular way. The Divine Ideas are always creating new avenues for you...listen... and have courage to pursue the ideas that come to you. This is true Divine Inspiration which will lead you to your pot of gold!

AFFIRMATIONS

I now allow in all of my good. Money flows to
me from multiple channels of the Universe.

I accept that money flows to me freely
and easily, and I allow it to happen.

I have complete faith and trust in this
invisible, unfailing, all providing Substance.
THERE IS NOTHING ELSE.

Today I release all fear, worry and concern of
my financial affairs and allow Substance to
fill every space in rich, appropriate form.

I have NO limitations on receiving money!
I accept it now and am deeply grateful for it!

TRAINING YOUR SUBCONSCIOUS SHIFTING THE PARADIGM

In order to truly start shifting to a more prosperous, abundant life, we must understand our subconscious mind and how it affects the amount of money we have or don't have.

It's all about our programming!

We have been programmed since childhood to believe in lack, limitation, and scarcity.

Look at our mass consciousness of society.. Every single day we hear and talk about the failing economy, no jobs, not enough money, not enough health care...and it goes on and on. Lack, lack, lack. We can't help but to buy into it ... we hear it every day, we participate in it and we begin to believe it. All of those words and thoughts just seep into our subconscious. We must train our minds to think of plenty instead. To think prosperous thoughts of riches, enough, and more!

Bob Proctor of "The Secret" says we must change the paradigm. What is paradigm? Nothing more than a multitude of belief patterns that you have been programmed with. The paradigm was formed with repetition. The ideas planted in your subconscious mind over and over again since birth!

Think of it this way. Since you were a baby, you have been programmed with thoughts and beliefs of others. Through *repetition*, you have received this programming all day, every day, all week, every week, all year, every year, till finally you're an adult with all this programming that's not serving you any more. Now, you must find a way to re-program those thoughts to positive, abundant, rich thoughts.

Your paradigm controls your results. It dictates your logic. It controls the amount of money you earn by your limited or unlimited beliefs. Remember the quote, "money flows to you as freely as your BELIEF allows it to happen." If you want more money in your life you must change your beliefs.

Your conscious mind, or reasoning mind will think things for you but its your subconscious mind that ultimately controls your perceptions, beliefs, and actions.

Here's the good news. Science now understands that the subconscious mind cannot differentiate between what's real and what's imagined. Your subconscious mind is wide open for you to put anything in it. Really think about this. What this is saying is that you can CONVINCE your mind that you are rich, that you have what you desire, and as a result, the physical evidence of it will show up. How do we do this? With daily affirmations of being rich, of having more, and repeating these affirmations over and over and over again until our subconscious mind is so SATURATED with these thoughts that it BELIEVES IT.

TRAINING YOUR SUBCONCIOUS IS NOTHING MORE THAN REPEATING RICH POWERFUL AFFIRMATIONS ON A CONTINUOUS BASIS.

Your brain is "hard-wired" to magnetically attract what you think about into your life. Remember, what you think about you bring about. What you focus on, you *become.*

When I lived in California, I often ventured to Venice Beach. The boardwalk on Venice Beach was a smorgasbord of artists, dancers, free thinkers, entertainers and quite colorful characters! I remember a particular character who daily set up a pile of sharp glass, chards of glass protruding through the pile, and proceeded to walk over it, unscathed without a scratch! It was as if he were walking on sand! At the time, this was something so foreign to me that my mind could not possibly wrap around the fact that this was real.

In later years, when I began studying spiritual principals and the power of the mind, I took a workshop that provided the opportunity to walk on fire. And walk, I did! This was a pivotal moment in my life when I truly did understand what powerful beings we are.

Have you ever done anything that proved the power of your mind? Have you ever healed yourself of something by thinking positive? Or talked yourself out of being sick, simply by accepting and believing only health for yourself? Or created something by affirming it to be so? Surely there are impossible feats that you've done, or even heard about. Like the mother who can lift her car to save the child underneath it, simply because she sets her mind to do so. We can all do amazing things...when we decide to believe and know it. This concept is no different in believing and attracting money. So having said this, let me challenge your mind with this.

If you could accept the idea that your monthly income is now tripled, what would you say? Would your mind say, "What? Are you crazy?"

If you can believe that you can walk on 1500 degree hot coals, or save a child under a car, or create or heal or..... fill in the blanks, why is it so difficult to believe that your money flows to you as *easily as your belief allows it to happen?* That your monthly income truly can triple if you decide that this is so!

Because of our programming! We've been taught at birth and all through our childhood about the lack of money. Our parents or teachers or other authority figures have told us that we can't "afford" or money doesn't grow on trees, or you have to struggle and work hard to earn money. It's ten times easier to wrap our minds around being able to walk on fire, etc. than it is to believe that money just flows to us. Why? Well, we never heard growing up that we couldn't walk on fire! I mean, did your parents ever say, "Don't you dare be thinking you can walk on fire! You're only five, now hush!!" Not in the programming!

But they did talk poverty, as society always does and has since the beginning of time! We've heard this for so long, and it's so deeply hidden and stuffed into our subconscious minds, that we have to change the programming, once and for all, to live more prosperous lives.

I am suggesting to you to find a way to change the paradigm of your subconscious mind. Change your patterns of belief.

Bob Proctor talks about how he dropped out of high school in the ninth grade. He eventually started his own business. He went from earning $4000 a year to earning $175,000 a year, IN A YEAR! He says that he became a millionaire by repeating this affirmation:

> *I am happy and grateful that my money now increases through multiple sources of the Universe on a continuous basis!*

He says that he repeated this affirmation over and over again, and when his money grew, he really didn't know how or why. In later years, he realized that his success was due to what he was "feeding" his subconscious mind.

The important thing is to find the exact words or phrases that evoke a powerful emotion within you, an emotion of excitement, joy, enthusiasm, and passion!

It's important to remember that the subconscious mind has no capacity to discern if something is true or false, real or unreal, good or bad. By nature, it only stores and acts upon the information given to it by the conscious mind.

Training your subconscious mind and shifting the paradigm will attract the things you desire, whether it is financial abundance, excellent health, fulfilling relationships and whatever you want to experience.

One of the things that I have heard people ask is "how do you have faith?"

Faith is a state of mind, and by repeating affirmations to your subconscious mind you are on your way to developing faith. Also, when your affirmations start showing up in your physical experience, your faith will grow by leaps and bounds!

Faith is the ability to SEE the invisible and BELIEVE the incredible.

You must CONVINCE the subconscious mind that you BELIEVE you will receive that which you ask. Your Faith will grow stronger as you apply these principles and see demonstrations of them.

ACT AS IF YOU ARE ALREADY IN POSSESSION OF THE MATERIAL THING YOU HAVE DEMANDED.

We are told, "Seek ye first the Kingdom of Heaven, and all things will be added unto you." What this is saying is that we must first have the consciousness of the thing we are desiring. The only way to change your life is to change your consciousness. To change your thoughts and to change your beliefs. We start by training our subconscious mind.

There are some wonderful tools that you can use to train the subconscious mind. One of the most powerful ways to train your subconscious mind is using a mental picture. Visualizing the thing that you desire. Nothing more than using the imagination!

First, you must get definite about your prosperity and what you desire. It's not enough that you should have a general desire for wealth. Everyone has that. But you must have a clear mental picture. If it's a new house, what does it look like? How many rooms does it have? Where is it located? What style is it? Give as many details as you can and hold that picture in your mind. Never lose sight of this picture.

Have you ever created a vision board? A vision board is a collection, or collage of pictures that you put together to tell the story of how you want your life to be. Daily focusing upon these pictures will impress upon our subconscious what we desire and again, with emotion and faith, will materialize it in to our physical world.

The purpose of the vision board is to "see" the images on the board and impress upon your subconscious mind these images. Once these images are programmed into our subconscious, they start showing up in our life! John Assaraf in the movie, "The Secret" talks about how he manifested his dream home by focusing on the vision board he created. Once again, this requires our imagination, and most importantly, our emotion of excitement and acting "as if" it is already ours. This may seem silly at first, but when you realize the power behind it, it will become your greatest asset.

The more clear and definite you make your picture, and the more you dwell upon it, bringing out all it's delightful details, the stronger your desire will be and the quicker your demonstrations will be.

The very first conversation that I had with the publishing consultant of this book, shared with me that she had just landed her job by using a vision board! She said that she created the board and within just a very short period of time of completing it, manifested a position with this particular publisher! Now, that's powerful!

You can also begin listening to subliminal tapes or CD's. Subliminal messaging is a method of sending messages directly to the subconscious mind, bypassing the more critical conscious, reasoning mind. Your prosperity has NOTHING to do with your reasoning mind. In fact, your reality is not what your eyes show your mind, but what your mind creates for your eyes to see!

Remember, your beliefs are just a result of your programming since birth. If subliminal messages are sent often enough to your subconscious, it will lead to a shift in your self beliefs.

You are just correcting your old thought and belief patterns through repetition. We are all exposed to subliminal messages every day due to the massive amounts of information we are exposed to.

By sending subliminal messages consistently to your subconscious mind, you can make positive changes in any area of your life, with absolutely NO effort required! Subliminal messages have been heralded as the keys to success by individuals such as Anthony Robbins and Bob Proctor.

Even if you simply record your own voice with powerful affirmations and listen to it three or four times a day, especially in the morning and at night, preferably before you go to sleep, you will find within a short time, your past thoughts and belief patterns disappearing rapidly. These tapes can be used for attracting money, acquiring better health, being more self confident, releasing phobias, attracting relationships, boosting your self esteem, treating illness or any other behavior or thought pattern you want to shift. The possibilities are endless.

Without question, your thoughts and thought patterns control your life. Your thoughts and beliefs determine if you have money or not!

One of the techniques that I have discovered and personally enjoy is called Mind Movies. This is a "movie" that you create using pictures, affirmations and music to create effective results to attract money, more meaningful relationships, health, success, creativity, and anything you wish to manifest. Its basically the same concept of using a vision board. But instead of cutting out images from magazines and pasting them on a board and just looking at them , Mind Movies uses images, affirmations and music that you create to make your very own personal movie.

The founder of Mind Movies had been trying to make a difference in his life. He had tried visualization and positive affirmations for some time, and had not had huge success. He wanted to make the art of visualization fun, and something that would elicit more of an emotional response. While searching the internet one day, he decided to make a movie on his computer of what he wanted his life to look like. Within 3 months of watching the movie he had created, he had achieved everything in it! This lead him on a quest to help as many people as possible, creating a downloadable software program of creating your own life movie.

The whole concept of mind movies, is that you are actually "seeing" your life as you want it, adding affirmations and music that evoke powerful emotions in you, and when this is played repeatedly over and over, your subconscious mind begins to accept these images as true. The creative process of making the movie is fun, and the results are astounding.

Just as we must nourish our body everyday with nutrition and exercise, we must also nourish our mind every day. Keep it attuned with rich, powerful thoughts and hold in consciousness the pictures of your desire.

Every morning when I first wake up, I decree that my day will be great! That my life is magical! That I love my life and am blessed for the people and circumstances in my life! I mentally image what I desire in my life and begin to get excited about it. I express my deep gratitude and appreciation for all of my desires and wants. This is a very powerful way to start your day. Decide right now how you want your day to be and set forth into motion this Creative Life Energy. Use your IMAGINATION, turn on the EMOTION, and have FAITH!

AFFIRMATIONS

I now allow the God mind to think through
me with rich appropriate thoughts.

There is nothing that I cannot be, do or have. I focus only
on what I desire, and that focus attracts it into my life.

I now choose to see my life the way I want it. This
mental picture activates the Life Force that begins
moving all things toward me and my desires.

I am happy and grateful that my money
now increases through multiple channels
of the Universe, on a consistent basis.

And all things, whatsoever ye shall ask in prayer,
believing, ye shall receive. Matthew 21:22

GIVE, GIVE, GIVE AND RECEIVE!
AS YOU TITHE...SO YOU PROSPER!

There is an ancient Law of Prosperity that says "True prosperity has a Spiritual basis. God Substance, is the source of your supply. Therefore you must do something definite and consistent to stay connected with that source. CONSISITENT giving opens the way to CONSISTENT receiving!"

By tithing, we partner with the Source and Substance from which all things come and open a channel for our good to pour forth.

The word "tithe" means "tenth" and is the magic number of increase.

I believe there are many misconceptions about tithing and in the lack of understanding it, many are not successful tithers. We try it and send our money, and say, "well nothing came back." But you have to understand that if you are giving to "get," that's trading, and a violation of the Law. We must learn to give with joy, not from a sense of obligation or duty, or guilt.

With tithing, or sharing, we should freely and joyfully give, whether it's our time, our service, or our money.

John Randolph Price states in "The Abundance Book:"

> *Giving is an esoteric science that never fails to produce results if it is done with love and joy, because the Law will shower you with a pressed down and multiplied return.*

The Universe will respond to us if we give from that spirit of generosity and love! Tithing is a practice of giving back to that which provides for you...and essentially opens up the unlimited channels to pour even more lavish abundance upon you!

Several years ago, I was a single mom and was just learning the principles of abundance and the benefits of tithing. I was sitting in church one Sunday and it came time for the prosperity basket to be passed. I sat there, with ten dollars to my name. That's it. Ten dollars. With an empty refrigerator, bills to be paid and my son to care for. I began to have the inner dialogue within myself...should I or shouldn't I? Do I tithe, or not? I began to ask Spirit for guidance. The basket is getting closer. I continued to pray. I informed the Divine Presence, that I would be happy to do whatever I was guided to do.

In that instant, I can only describe to you that what I felt was an all-encompassing peace. My whole being was filled with love and I knew, I absolutely *knew* that everything would be alright and I would be taken care of. I didn't know how, I just knew this as Truth.

The basket passed by me and my ten dollars *happily* landed in it.

Later, after church, I went to my post office box to check my mail. I opened my box, and in it was a plain, white envelope with no return address on it. The writing on it looked like a six year old's scribble. My curiosity was piqued! I opened the envelope and in it contained twenty five dollars cash! No note, no nothing. Just $25. I was in awe! And then in tears of gratitude.

But the story didn't stop there. Later that afternoon, I visited some friends. I began to relay my story to them and the miracle that had followed. As I was leaving, they proceeded to hand me twenty five dollars because they were so inspired by the story I had told, they felt moved to tithe to me!

Little did I know that day, that by giving the last few dollars that I owned, in faith, that my money would be more that doubled by the end of the day. Ten dollars became fifty, magically, effortlessly!

I still possess that envelope to this day. It has been a wonderful reminder and teacher for me, anytime I dare to entertain thoughts of doubt or worry.

In Catherine Ponder's book, "The Dynamic Laws of Prosperity", she writes:

> *Do not try to reason through the mysterious power of tithing. Instead, simply accept the fact that tithing releases a mystical power to prosper you. When you tithe first, before paying bills or meeting other financial obligations, you will find that the remaining 90 percent of your income goes much further!*

Tithing is an act of FAITH that activates rich Substance to prosper and expand your wealth in ways you can't imagine!

We must become as little children. We must learn to "Let go and let God." We've all heard this before. But it is a powerful Truth. Children do not worry about what will happen tomorrow. They do not sit and worry or have any thought about being fed, or cared for in any way. It's just a "given." Can you imagine never having any worry or fear, and taking on the attitude that it's just a "given" that we will have all that we need and desire? But this is an ABSOLUTE TRUTH! We *are* that taken care of! The Universe has our back! Our only requirement is faith!

If we lived as a child, in perpetual trust.... We would be living the true Spiritual Essence of who we are...in all our glory and love and power and wisdom, and light and joy and passion and play and wholeness and fullness, and magnificence!

So again, we are directed to take an action that requires faith.

Tithing is an opportunity to do just that. It is also an opportunity to give to *yourself.* We are taught that we are One with God. In the I AM of our awareness of Being, of our God Self, if we are giving to God, we are, in essence, giving to our Self. By giving *anything*, our money, our time, or our love, we are giving to our self because that is exactly what comes back to us by Law of Attraction.

The more you practice this important Law of Sharing, and you begin to experience it's results as more money begins flowing to you, you will be happy to say "thank you" by giving ten percent of all money that you have received. Begin now to practice this important step. You will discover for yourself that tithing is the best investment you can make for your financial success.

AFFIRMATIONS

I gladly give with an open and loving heart and know
that my abundance returns to me, multiplied.

As I freely and lovingly give, I freely and lovingly receive.

I release all fear and worry from sharing my money,
knowing my supply is endless.

By blessing all that I have, and sharing a tenth of all I
receive, I increase the Law of Abundance in my life.

Bring ye the tithes into the store house, that there may be
meat in mine house, and prove me now herewith, saith
the Lord of hosts, if I will not open you the windows
of heaven and pour you out a blessing, that there shall
not be room enough to receive it. Malachi 3:10

CONCLUSION

Before you can begin to put any of these principles to successful use, your mind must be open to *accept* your riches. It begins with clearing out all INDECISION, DOUBT AND FEAR. This may require looking deep within yourself and at the beliefs and patterns that have determined your life to this point.

In the beginnings of creating this formula and while writing this book, I was in the middle of divorce, I did not have a home, (I was staying with friends) I did not have a steady income, and a few months earlier my son left home to become a Marine. For the first time in twenty years, I found my self alone and saying to myself, "now what?"

It was time for me to take a look at the relationships that were not working, and the past patterns of beliefs that were not serving me. I began to understand that what was required was something that I needed to change about *myself.*

In working with the "cause" that had attracted unwanted experiences in my life, including low self esteem, self criticism, blame, fear, self doubts, and excuses, and by focusing only on the Presence of Love within me, and my direct connection to this Living Presence that serves as our Divine Partner, this formula was "born," and the floodgates opened up and the good rushed in! And once things began shifting, it shifted quickly, so quickly, that it took me by surprise!

I realized that those experiences and relationships in my past had all played an important role in helping me to *define* who I AM and what I desire in my life.

I realized that by changing the limiting beliefs that I had held, my abundance (including money) started pouring in, in ways that I never would have imagined.

I share these things, because I am very clear that the beliefs that we have held about ourselves for so long, have to be let go of before we can truly manifest money or any thing else good in our life.

The simple matter is if we deleted all thoughts and emotions of fear, worry, doubt, shame, greed, resentment, hatred, jealousy, and anger, and lived in a state of love and acceptance for ourselves and all of humanity....we would truly be 'enlightened' and live a life of luxury, completeness, and wholeness.

Throughout this book we have discussed the steps towards manifesting our riches. Many will read this book and make the excuses; "but I don't have any money in the bank, or, I'm on welfare...or my job doesn't pay very well...or I don't have time...or my spouse won't let me... or I'm afraid of what others will think...or I don't have the right education, or the talent, I don't know the right people," and on and on.

BEGIN WHERE YOU ARE RIGHT NOW....WHAT A PERFECT PLACE TO BE!

Make the decision right now, today, to accept for yourself that you are a rich, prosperous, Spiritual being. Have faith that there is an invisible force at work for you, waiting for you to get definite about your desire. This all providing Substance, this Life Force Energy ALWAYS says, "YES!" to your desire and to your good! This invisible Intelligence is waiting on tiptoe for you to "get" that YOU hold the power.

Allow this power to flow through you and for you, and with constant affirmations, SEE, FEEL and BELIEVE yourself already in possession of the money and expect it to appear in your physical experience. You don't have to know the HOW. That's not your job. Your job is to have faith and take action if you are inspired to do so.

You must form a clear, mental picture of the thing you wish to have, do or become. Hold this mental image in your thoughts constantly, while expressing deep gratitude to this Formless Substance that all your desires are granted.

The following is adopted from Napoleon Hill's, "Think And Grow Rich" and is an exercise in setting you on your way to financial freedom.

1) Fix in your mind the *exact* amount of money you desire.
2) Decide what you intend to give in return for the money you desire.
3) Establish a definite date when you intend to possess the money you desire.
4) Create a definite plan for carrying out your desire and begin at once!
5) Write out a clear, precise statement of the amount of money you intend to acquire, name the time limit of its acquisition, state what you intend to give in return, and describe clearly the plan through which you intend to accumulate it.
6) Read your written statement aloud twice daily, once in the morning and once in the evening.

As you read, SEE and FEEL and BELIEVE yourself already in possession of the money. Do not waiver. Do not give up until you have a breakthrough and a demonstration.

Little did I realize, when I began working with the power of prosperous thinking, how much my own life could change as I developed and wrote down the ideas in this book!

Regardless of what life has dealt you in the past, your current financial situation, what relationships you have attracted, or what limitations you may have decreed for yourself, as you begin to understand and practice the principles in this book, you will begin to experience a feeling of expansion. Your life may shift dramatically as your good begins to show up in physical form. Have courage and accept your success as it comes rushing in.

In this deep expanded consciousness, and as the shifts begin to take place in your life, you will realize that the real value is not money itself.

The real value is your awareness and connection with this Living Presence and the knowledge that it is always in the formless, waiting for your understanding of it, to bring it into physical manifestation by your belief in it and your demand upon it.

The real value is that you now know that the path to financial abundance is simply one of BELIEF, HAPPINESS, and FAITH. That financial abundance does not occur because of one's good luck, hard work, or struggle. Abundance is simply the Universe's response to thoughts and FEELINGS of abundance! When we are able to accomplish the feeling of abundance BEFORE the physical evidence shows up, we have the SECRET to attracting money.

The real value is that you realize that nothing keeps you from your wealth, that it is not now, nor has it ever been something outside of you. Now you are on your way to a freedom far greater than you have ever known.

I am happy and grateful to share the principles in this book and know that this is just the beginning of your own journey of enrichment and fulfillment.

Be prosperous and free.

GUIDED MEDITATION

I open my heart and mind now to the mind of God. I now allow this God mind to think through me . I let go of all thoughts of the past and all limitations. I know that my good now expresses through me as I open myself up to this Divine presence of All-Providing Substance. I consciously become aware of the Oneness of this Supreme Intelligence and allow its fullness and richness. I allow this Living Presence to expand through me, "as" me, as it expresses its infinite riches through my life. I feel this Oneness with the all of all that is everything, everywhere, in every space, at all times. And in this state of fullness, I decide.

I decide right now to be abundant. I choose to acknowledge my power as a Spiritual Being. I get definite about my prosperity and command my good and my desires to come forth. I allow this Substance to flow into all of my financial affairs. Thank you universe for your support in my decision. Thank you Substance, as I pour all my faith in to you. I rely only on this all providing Substance, this Living Presence, to supply me with riches of all kinds. I know that I am one with all that exists.

I image for myself all good things. I see myself as rich and fulfilled. With great happiness and excitement I allow my riches to flow and appear in physical manifestation. This never ending all providing stream of good flows to me from multiple channels of the Universe. There is plenty, plenty, plenty! I am happy and grateful that my money now increases through these channels. I am enthusiastic, excited and passionate about living a life that I get to create! I now choose absolute and continuous abundance. I know with all my soul that I AM the creator of my life. I accept this Truth with renewed faith and enthusiasm. I expect my good and with deep gratitude I remain strong and constant in my faith, therefore, this Formless Substance remains strong and constant in my life. I appreciate this never ending flow of money, of love, of happiness, of health, of harmonious relationships and perfect self expression.

I AM happy. I AM loved. I AM free.

And so it is!

RESOURCES

Books

The Abundance Book - John Randolph Price
Dare to Prosper - Catherine Ponder
Prosperity - Charles Fillmore, Founder of Unity
The Power of Intention - Dr. Wayne Dyer
Think and Grow Rich - Napoleon Hill
The Dynamic Laws of Prosperity - Catherine Ponder
The Science of Getting Rich - Wallace Wattles
Dialogue On Awakening, Communion with a Loving
    Brother - Tom Carpenter

Websites

www.mindmovies.com
www.realsubliminal.com

I invite you to write to me and share your results of implementing this formula and I look forward to hearing of your success!

Susie Greene
P.O. Box 17674
Asheville, NC 28816